TWILIGHT RHYTHMS & OTHER
POEMS

CHARLES REZNIKOFF

FORGOTTEN POETS

Editor | Dick Whyte   Number 11 | 2022

CHARLES REZNIKOFF (1894-1976) was born in the Jewish neighborhood of Brownsville in Brooklyn, New York, after his parents left Russia, fleeing the anti-Jewish pogroms during the 1800s. Reznikoff excelled in school, and started university 3 years ahead of his peers, first in Missouri studying journalism, and then in New York studying law. Reznikoff began writing poetry as a teen, and under the influence of Imagism gravitated toward "haiku-like" forms – compressed, fragmented, suggestive – and 'free verse'. In the late-1910s and 1920s he self-published numerous collections, but had trouble finding support for his work. Besides poetry, Reznikoff wrote a number of plays and novels, also to little success. In the 1930s he was a part of the Objectivist movement, led by Louis Zukofsky, who saw Reznikoff's work as a leading light in English-language poetry. Despite this, his verse remained largely ignored. To make ends meet Reznikoff worked briefly as a lawyer, as a salesperson for his father's hat company, and then as a freelance writer and editor. Just before his death Reznikoff's complete poems were re-published, making them available to a new generation of poets, including the Beats, and in particular Allen Ginsberg, who affectionally referred to him as one of "Walt Whitman's grandchildren."

Selections from *Rhythms* (self-published, 1918); *Rhythms II* (self-published, 1919); *Poems* (Samuel Roth at the New York Poetry Bookshop, 1920; containing revisions of *Rhythms*, & *Rhythms II*, & a third group of poems); *Uriel Acosta: A Play & A Fourth Group of Verse* (self-published, 1921); and *Five Groups of Verse* (self-published, 1927). In each subsequent publication Reznikoff revised the verses many times; this collection draws primarily on versions from *Poems* (1920) and *Five Groups of Verse* (1927).

Cover: Coulton Waugh - 'Untitled Drawings' (*The Plowshare*, June 1917). Frontispieces: 'Reading Chairs' (*The Savitar: Published by the Junior Class of the University of Missouri*, 1911) & Zavado – 'Portrait' (*Coterie*, Winter 1920-21). Inside: Coulton Waugh - assorted drawings & woodcuts (*Bruno's Weekly*, 1915-16), etc.

FORGOTTEN PRESS
Aotearoa | New Zealand

ISBN: 978-1-991310-20-0 (paperback) • 978-1-991310-21-7 (hardback)
978-1-991310-22-4 (ebook)

CHARLES REZNIKOFF
TWILIGHT RHYTHMS & OTHER POEMS

Selections from:

RHYTHMS I & II
(1918 | 1919)

POEMS
(1920)

A 4TH & 5TH GROUP OF VERSE
(1921 | 1927)

FORGOTTEN POETS

edited by **Dick Whyte**.

Missing Meters! Lost Lyrics!
Vanished Verses!

LEWIS ALEXANDER
PEARL ANDELSON
IRIS BARRY
GWENDOLYN BENNETT
ADELAIDE CRAPSEY
MARY CAROLYN DAVIES
HILDA DOOLITTLE
HILDEGARDE FLANNER
F.S. FLINT
JUN FUJITA
SADAKICHI HARTMANN
T.E. HULME
TAKEKO KUJO
AMY LOWELL
MINA LOY
YONE NOGUCHI
CHARLES REZNIKOFF
EDWARD STORER
MARIE TUDOR-GARLAND
AKIKO YOSHINO
AKIKO YANAGIWARA
& MANY MORE

FORGOTTENPOETS.COM

POEMS

BY

CHARLES REZNIKOFF

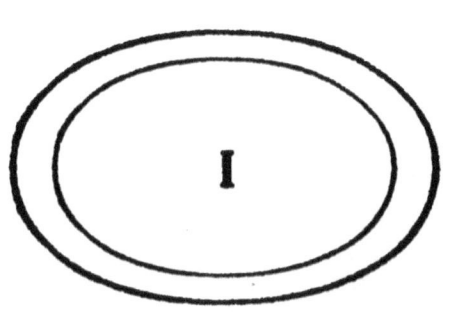

I

THE stars are hidden,
The lights are out;
The tall black houses
Are ranked about.

I beat my fists
On the stout doors,
No answering steps
Come down the floors.

I have walked until
I am faint and numb;
From one dark street
To another I come.

The comforting
Winds are still.

This is a chaos
Through which I stumble.
Till I reach the void
And down I tumble.

The stars will then
Be out forever;
The fists unclenched,
The feet walk never

And all I say
Blown by the wind
Away.

THE shopgirls leave their work
Quietly.

Machines are still, tables and chairs
Darken.

The silent rounds of mice and roaches begin.

THE dead are walking silently.

I sank them six feet underground,
The dead are walking and no sound.

I raised on each a brown hill,
The dead are walking slow and still.

ON Brooklyn Bridge I saw a man drop dead.
It meant no more than if he were a sparrow.

Above us rose Manhattan;
Below, the river spread to meet sea and sky.

THE dead man lies in the street.
They spread a sack over his bleeding head.
It drizzles. Gutter and walks are black.

His wife now at her window,
The supper done, the table set,
Waits for his coming out of the wet.

So one day, tired of the sky and host of stars,
  I'll thrust the tinsel by.

Her kindliness is like the sun
Toward dusk shining through a tree.

Her understanding is like the sun,
Shining through mist on a width of sea.

I STEP into the fishy pool
As if into a cool
Vault.
I, too, become
Cold-blooded, dumb.

WRINGING, wringing his pierced hands,
He walks in a wood where once a flood
Washed the ground into loose white sand;
And the trees stand each a twisted cross,
Smooth and white with loss of leaves and bark,
Together like warped yards and masts
Of a fleet at anchor centuries.

No blasts come to the hollow of these dead;
Long since the water has gone from the stony bed.
No fields and streets for him, his pathway runs
Among these skeletons, through these white sands,
Wringing, wringing his pierced hands.

HAIR and faces glossy with sweat in August
At night through narrow streets glaring with lights
People as if in funeral processions;

On stoops weeds in stagnant pools,
At windows waiting for a wind that never comes.
Only, a lidless eye, the sun again.

No one else in the street but a wind blowing,
Store-lamps dimmed behind frosted panes,
Stars, like the sun broken and scattered in bits.

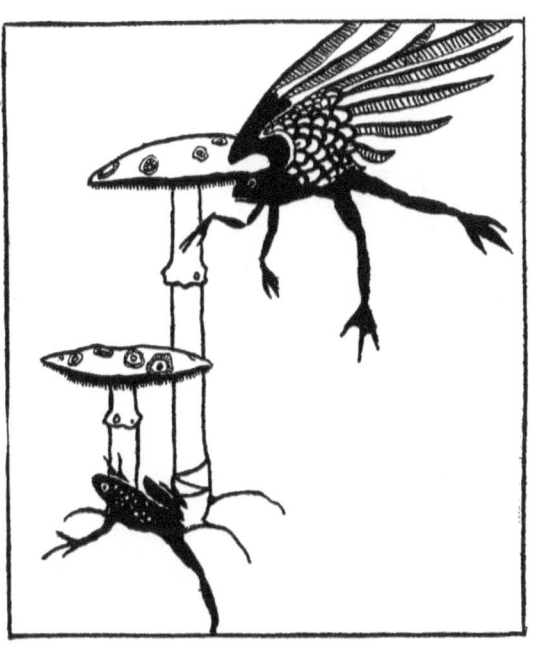

I WALKED through the lonely marsh
Among the white birches.

Above the birches rose
Three crows,
Croaking, croaking.

The trumpets blare war
And the streets are filled with echoes.

HOW shall we mourn you who are killed
and wasted,
Sure that you would not die with your
work unended,
As if the iron scythe in the grass stops
for a flower?

THEY dug her grave so deep
No voice can creep to her.

She can feel no stir
Of joy when her girl sings,

And quietly she lies
When her girl cries.

THE troopers are riding, are riding by,
The troopers are riding to kill and die
That a clean flag may cleanly fly.

They touch the dust in their homes no more,
They are clean of the dirt of shop and store,
And they ride out clean to war.

MY work done, I lean on the window-sill,
Watching the dripping trees.

The rain is over, the wet pavement shines.
From the bare twigs
Rows of drops like shining buds are hanging.

THE fingers of your thoughts
Are moulding your face
Ceaselessly.

The wavelets of your thoughts
Are washing your face
Beautiful.

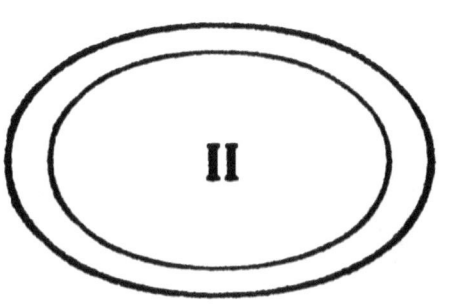

II

I HAVE not even been in the fields,
Nor lain my fill in the soft foam,
And here you come blowing, cold wind.

BEGGARS about the streets
Pray to God between set teeth.

Up by star and star
Until the outer frozen blackness,

Down the earth between stones
Until black rocks in ledge on ledge.

ON the kitchen shelf the dusty medicine bottles;
She in her room heaped under a sheet,
And men and women coming in with clumsy steps.

STUBBORN flies buzzing
In the morning when she wakes.

The flat roofs, higher, lower,
Chimneys, water-tanks, cornices.

Epidemic

STREAMERS of crepe idling before doors.

The Idiot

WITH green stagnant eyes,
Arms and legs
Loose ends of string in a wind,

Keep smiling at your father.

Vaudeville

I LEAVE the theatre,
Keeping step, keeping step to the music.
It sticks to my feet,
Stepped into dung.

    Night falls
        In still flakes.

In the Ghetto

THE winter afternoon darkens.
The shoemaker bends close to the shoe,
His hammer raps faster.

An old woman waits,
Rubbing the cold from her hands.

IN the shop she, her mother, and grandmother,
Thinking at times of women at windows
    in still streets,
Or women reading, a glow on resting hands.

SHE who worked patiently,
Her children grown,
Lies in her grave patiently.

SHADOWS, mice whisk over the unswept floor,
Tumble through rustling papers.

Squeeze into desk drawers,
Biting the paper into yellowed flakes
And leaving crumbs of filth.

I KNOCKED. A strange voice answered.
So they, too, have moved away.

We had walked up and down the block
     many times
          Until alone.

I wonder where they have moved to.

Scrubwoman

ONE shoulder lower,
With unsure step like a bear erect,
The smell of the wet black rags
    that she cleans with about her.

Scratching with four stiff fingers
    her half-bald head,
        Smiling.

The Park In Winter

IT rains.
The elms curve into clouds of twigs.
The lawns are empty.

DARK early and only the river shines
Like grey ice, the ships moored fast.

WE heard no step in the hall.
She came
Sudden as a rainbow.

THE sandwiches are elaborate affairs:
Toast, bacon, toast, chicken, toast.

We sip our coffee watching the rouged women
Walk quickly to their seats, unsmiling,
    contemptuous.

THE water broke on the slope of her hips
And foamed about her,
The slender moon stood in the blue heavens.

THE imperious dawn comes
To the clink of milk bottles
And round-shouldered sparrows twittering.

LIKE a curtain turning in an open window.

Like a swan effortless
On a lake shaded and still in summer,
Dipping a white neck in the trees' shadow,
Hardly beating the water with golden feet.

    Sorrow before her
Was gone like noise from a street,
       Snow falling.

THE horses keep tossing their heads and
    stamp the hollow flooring,
Wheel knocks into wheel
As the ferry glides out into a damp wind.

The coal-truck horses, three abreast,
    ponderously,
Sides and rumps shaking.

With blown manes and tails
The horses fling themselves along
    lifting their riders.

The thin horses step beside the lawns
    in the park,
The small hoofs newly oiled,
Heads high, their red nostrils taking the air.

Twilight

No stars
In the blue curve
Of the heavens,
No wind.

Far off,
A white horse
In the green gloom
Of the meadow.

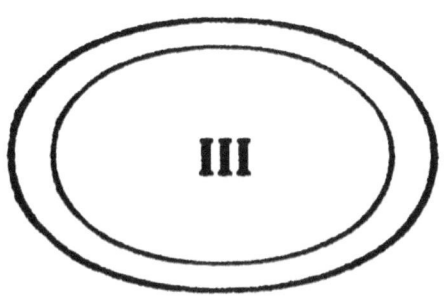

III

THE twigs tinge the winter sky
Brown.

THE house-wreckers have left the door
    and a staircase,
Now leading to the empty room of night.

THE sun was low over the blue morning water;
The waves of the bay were silent on the
    smooth beach,
Where in the night the silver fish had
    died gasping.

OLD men and boys search the wet
        garbage with fingers
And slip pieces in bags.

This fat old man has found the hard
        end of a bread
            And bites it.

THE pedlar who goes from shop to shop,
Has seated himself on the stairs
    in the dim hallway,
And the basket of apples upon his knees,
    breathes the odour.

THE girls outshout the machines
And she strains for their words, blushing.

Soon she, too, will speak
Their speeches glibly.

HER work was to count linings—
The day's seconds in dozens.

THEY have built red factories along
  Lake Michigan,
And the purple refuse coils like congers
  in the green depths.

I WALKED in a street, head high,
When a thug began beating a passer-by.

I gave no help with blow or cry,
But hurried on glad it wasn't I.

SHOWING a torn sleeve, with stiff
    and shaking fingers the old man
Pulls off a bit of the baked apple,
    shiny with sugar,
Eating with reverence food,
    the great comforter.

A CLERK tiptoeing the office floor
In a flurry of insignificant stuff;
Or with samples from store to store
To speak politely to the gruff,
Entering timidly the door,
Trying to bow and smile it right
With smiles seen not true enough,
A young man who was so bright.

They spoke proudly and well,
Fearing and revering none,
Had no longing to buy and sell
Or chatter with girls half the night;
What at last have these men done,
The young men who were so bright?

STILL much to read, but too late.
I turn out the light.

The leaves of the tree are green beside
    the street-lamp;
The wind hardly blows and the tree
    makes no noise.

Tomorrow up early,
The crowded street-car, the factory.

A SLENDER tree, alone in the fields,
Between the roofs of the town and the woods
    like a low hill.

In the open
The birds are faintly overheard.

A u g u s t

THE city breaks in houses to the sea,
    uneasy with waves.
In the streets truck-horses, muscles sliding
    under the steaming hides,
Pound the sparks flying about their hoofs.

ON the shaken water
Of the shining sea
We lay like seaweed
Carelessly.

Afterwards running
With outstretched hands
We chase each other
Across the sands.

STEAM-SHOVEL, in the hollow where yard
    and poplars were,
Going home we would look at the rows
    of poplars.

IN the streets children beneath tall houses
    at games greedily,
Remembering clocks, the house-cats
    lapping time.

SPEAKING and speaking again words
    like silver bubbles,
We walk at dusk through rain.

The sky has grown black with a tinge of red
    from the street-lamps;
Triangular pools form in the square cracks
    of the pavement,
        Noisy with rain.

TREES standing far off in winter
Against a polished blue sky
With boughs blown about like brown hair;

The stiff lines of the twigs
Blurred by the April buds;

Or branches crowded with leaves
And a wind turning
Their dark green light.

SHIPS dragged into the opaque green
    of the sea,
Visible winds flinging houses apart—
And here the poplar roots lifting
    the pavement an inch.

SHE woke at a child crying
And turned to the empty cradle,
Forgetting.

UNDER the heavens furrowed with clouds
A man behind his stumbling plough.

KITTEN, pressed into a rude shape
    by cart wheels,
An end to your slinking away and trying
    to hide behind ash-cans.

SUDDENLY we noticed that we were
    in darkness;
So we went into the house
    and lit the lamp.

The talk fell apart and bit by bit
    slid into a lake.
At last we rose and bidding each other
    good night went to our rooms.

In and about the house darkness lay,
    a black fog;
And each on his bed spoke to himself
    alone, making no sound.

Ghetto Funeral

FOLLOWED by his lodge, shabby men
    stumbling over the cobblestones,
And his children, faces red and ugly with tears,
    eyes and eyelids red,
In the black coffin in the black hearse
    the old man.

No longer secretly grieving
That his children are not strong enough
    to go the way he wanted to go
And was not strong enough.

THE baby woke with curved, confiding fingers.
The gas had been turned down until it was
    only a yellow glimmer.
A rat walked slowly from under the washtub.

THE rain fell and stopped but the clouds stayed
Over the warehouses lonely at night.

A man in the street went mumbling to himself,
Screeched.
Then walked on mumbling to himself
Between the warehouses.

SHE sat by the window opening into the airshaft,
And looked across the parapet
At the new moon.
She would have taken the hairpins out of her
    carefully coiled hair,
And thrown herself on the bed in tears;
But he was coming and her mouth had to be
    pinned into a smile.

If he would have her, she would marry
    whatever he was,
She who, slim and gentle once, would soon
    become clumsy, talking harshly.
A knock. She lit the gas and opened her door.
Her aunt and the man—skin loose under his eyes,
    the face slashed with wrinkles.
"Come in," she said as gently as she could
    and smiled.

THE house was pitch-dark.
He entered his room. Books and papers were
    heaped over the floor.
He stuck the candle in a corner, and on his
    knees began to go through the papers.
He must finish that night: the next day
    the others would move in.
Yes, here was the bold handwriting, the bundle
    of letters tied together.
He took these into the kitchen. He did not
    need a light:
He ought to know the way, had walked it
    so often.

He crammed all into the stove and lit a match.
The fire ran over the surface and died out.
He tore the letters into bits and lit match
    after match,
Until nothing was left but brown pieces
    with black, crumbled edges.

As the papers twisted and opened, tormented
    by fire,
Darling had stood out in the writing against
    the flame
For a moment before the ink was grey on
    black ash that fell apart.

Here was the bedroom where she had been sick.
Her teeth fell out; before the end her nose
    rotted off.

He uncovered a bunch of dried flowers
    and white gauze—
Her bridal veil and bouquet left in the rubbish.
He went back to the kitchen stove.
    The gauze flew up in a great flame,
    flowers remained—blackened stalks.
Now he was through. He closed door after door
    softly behind him.

FROM where she lay she could see the snow
    crossing the darkness slowly,
Thick about the arc-lights like moths in summer.

She could just move her head.
    She had been lying so for months.
Her son was growing tall and broad-shouldered,
    his face becoming like that of her father,
Dead now for years.

She lay under the bed-clothes as if she, too,
    were covered with snow,
Calm, facing the blackness of night,
Through which the snow fell in the crowded
    movement of stars.
Dead, nailed in a box, her son was being sent to her,
Through fields and cities cold and white with snow.

HOUR after hour in a rocking-chair
    on the porch,
Hearing the wind in the shade trees.

At times a storm comes up and the dust
    is blown in long curves along the street,
Over the carts driven slowly, drivers and
    horses nodding.

Years are thrown away as if I were immortal,
The nights spent in talking
Shining words, sometimes, like fireflies
    in the darkness—
Lighting and going out and after all no light.

TREES shrugging their shoulders in the wind
And the ceaseless weaving of the uneven water.

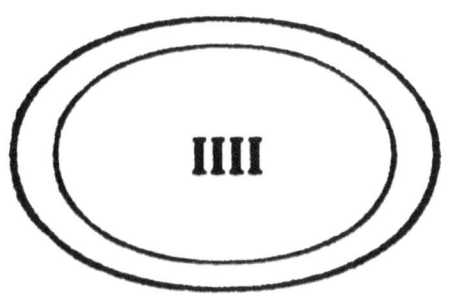

IIII

April

THE stiff lines of the twigs
Blurred by buds.

A p h r o d i t e   V r a n i a

THE ceaseless weaving of the uneven water.

M o o n l i t   N i g h t

THE trees' shadows lie in black pools on the lawns.

WHEN I was four years old my mother
    led me to the park.
The spring sunshine was not too warm.
    The street was almost empty.
The witch in my fairy book came
    walking along.
She stooped to fish mouldy grapes out
    of the gutter.

WE children used to cross the orchard,
the brown earth covered with little green apples,
Into the field beyond;
The grass came up over our knees,
There were so many flowers we did not care
    to pick any—

Daisies and yellow daisies, golden-rod
    and buttercups.
Is was so hot the field smelt of cake baking.

IT had long been dark, though still an hour
    before supper-time.
The boy stood at the window behind
    the curtain.
The street under the black sky was bluish
    white with snow.
Across the street, where the lot sloped
    to the pavement,
Boys and girls were going down on sleds.
The boys were after him because he was a Jew.

At last his father and mother slept.
    He got up and dressed.
In the hall he took his sled and went
    out on tiptoe.
No one was in the street. The slide was
worn smooth and slippery—just right.
He laid himself on the sled and shot away.
He went down only twice.

He stood knee-deep in snow:
No one was in the street, the windows
    were darkened;
Those near the street-lamps were ashine,
but the rooms inside were dark;
On the street were long shadows
    of clods of snow.
He took his sled and went back into
    the house.

Sunday Walks
In The Suburbs

OVER stones mossed with hot dust,
　　no shade but the thin, useless
　　shadows of roadside grasses;
Into the wood's gloom, staring back
　　at the blue flowers on stalks
　　　　thin as threads.

The green slime—a thicket of young trees
　　standing in brown water;
With knobs like muscles, a naked tree
　　stretches up,
Dead; and a dead duck, head sunk in the
　　water, as if diving.

　　The tide is out.
Only a pool is left on the creek's stinking mud.
Someone has thrown a washboiler away.
On the bank a heap of cans;
Rats, covered with rust, creep in and out.
The white edges of the clouds
　　like veining in a stone.

AFTER dinner, Sunday afternoon, we boys
    would walk slowly
To the lots between the streets and the marshes;
And seated under the pale blue cloudless sky
    would watch the ball game—
In a noisy, joyous crowd, lemonade men
    out in the fringe, tinkling their bells
        beside their yellow carts.
As we walked back, the city stretched its rows
    of houses across the lots—
Light after light, as the lamplighter
    went his way and women lit the gas
        in kitchens to make supper.

AT night, after the day's work, he wrote.
Year after year he had written, but the
right words were still not all there,
the right rhythms not always used.
He corrected the old and added new.

While away on a business trip he died.
His children playing about the house, left
home by the widow out at work, found the
manuscript so carefully written
        and rewritten.

The paper was good to scribble on.
Then they tore it into bits.
At night the mother came home
        and swept it out.

AT six o'clock it was pitch-dark.
It might have been after midnight in the city
    and no lamps lit along the streets.
He would have liked to hide in the city from
    that sky of stars.
Beside bushes and thin, leafless trees he
    walked upon the frozen clods and ruts.
There was no wind across that blackness
    of fields and lakes;
Only the sound of his own feet knocking
    on the road.
There the stars were poured, and there
    scattered. He thought,
The symmetry in growth and life on earth,
    our sense of order, is not
        controlling in the universe.

ALL night the wind blew.
In the morning the deck-hands
Were running around to warm up.
The boat rose and fell
On the little waves.
Now and then it hit
A chopping wave.
The wind blew the white caps
    of the water
Into spray.
Far off the wild geese
Were flying over the lake.

The lake was ridged with waves,
Rolling between the shores.
The northern shore was cliff,
Barren of houses or trees;
On the flat southern shore
Towns spread out like patches.

There was no rest from the wind:
It blew steadily colder.
The deck-hands ran about,
Beating their arms over their breasts.
The wild geese far away
Were flying south in squads.

SCARED dogs looking backwards with
        patient eyes;
At windows stooping old women, wrapped
        in shawls;
Old men, wrinkled as knuckles, on the stoops.

A bitch, backbone and ribs showing
        in the sinuous back,
Sniffed for food, her swollen udder nearly
        rubbing along the pavement.

Once a toothless woman opened her door,
Chewing a slice of bacon that hung
        from her mouth like a tongue.

This is where I walked night after night;
This is where I walked away many years.

SWIFTLY the dawn became day.
   I went into the street.
Loudly and cheerfully the sparrows chirped.
The street-lamps were still lit, the sky pale
   and brightening.
Hidden in trees and on the roofs,
Loudly and cheerfully the sparrows chirped.

THIS noise in the subway will sound no louder
    than the wind in trees;
You, too, will be used to it.
    After a while you will forget to care
        Whether you ride in subways or on horses.

Railway Station
At Cleveland

UNDER cloud on cloud the lake is black;
Wheeling locomotives in the yard
Pour their smoke into the crowded sky.

Office Help

MORNING after morning the sun shone.

    She kept making her entries
    Until the street
    Filled with twilight.

BETWEEN factories grease coils along the river.
Tugs drag their guts of smoke,
    like beetles stepped on.

IN the even curves of gutters and even
    curves of gutters
The irregular slope of the park's barren hill.

OUT of the hills the trees bulge;
The sky hangs in lumps of cloud.

SPARROWS scream at the dawn one note:

How should they learn melody
In the street's noises?

Evening

THE trees in the windless field like a herd asleep.

Indian Summer

THE men in the field are almost through stacking
    rows of pale yellow cornstalks.
On the lawn a girl is raking the leaves into a fire.

Visiting

I

ALMOST midnight. "Good night."
   "Good night."
I close the heavy door behind me.
The black courtyard smells of water:
   it has been raining.
What were we talking about?

II

He leans back along the sofa. I talk.
   His fingers twitch at his bath-robe.
I talk. I turn my pockets inside out.
In his oblique eyes a polite disdain.

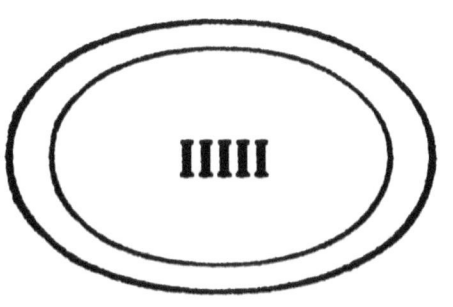

IIIII

I CHARGE you, lips and teeth,
Keep watch upon my tongue:
Silence is legal tender everywhere.

I HAVE a quarrel with the clock.
Quick, quick!
These inconsiderable seconds fill
The basins of our lives to overflowing,
And we are emptied
Into the sink and pipes of death.
How furiously it ticks this fine morning.
Sun, of all that lived God has only
    listened to Joshua,
How shall I hope that He will listen to me?

David

THE shadow that does not leave my feet,
How shrunken now it lies;
With sunshine I am anointed king,
I leap before the ark, I sing;
I seem to walk but I dance about,
You think me silent but I shout.

A Citizen

I KNOW little about bushes and trees,
I have met them in backyards and streets;
I shall become disreputable if I hang about them.
Yet to see them comforts me,
When I think of my life as snarled.
Was not knowledge first on trees?

Dawn

NO-ONE is on the lawn so early but the birds,
Sparrows and robins pecking at the seeds
The wind has blown here; the wind itself is gone.

Autumn Night

THE asphalt winds in and out
About the trees, the lawns, the lake;
A thousand lights shine among the trees,
And in the circles underneath
The grass is brightly green;
But all these lights do not warm the wind.

FROM the fog a gull flies slowly
And is lost in fog. The buildings are only clouds.

I HAVE learnt the Hebrew blessing
    before eating bread;
Is there no blessing before reading Hebrew?

MY thoughts have become like ancient Hebrew
In two tenses only, past and future—
    I was and I shall be with you.

HOW difficult for me is Hebrew:
Even the Hebrew for *mother*, for *bread*, for *sun*
    Is foreign.
    How far have I been exiled, Zion.

How miserly this bush is:
Why do you crouch behind a fence,
Holding on to your little copper leaves?

Have you no faith in spring?

THE sun shone into the bare, wet tree;
It became a pyramid of criss-cross lights,
And in each corner the light nested.

AFTER I had worked all day at what
    I earn my living, I was tired.
Now my own work has lost another day,
I thought, but began slowly,
And slowly my strength came back to me.
Surely, the tide comes in twice a day.

Building Boom

THE avenue of willows leads nowhere:
It begins at the blank wall of a new
    apartment house
And ends in the middle of a lot for sale.
Papers and cans are thrown about the trees.
The disorder does not touch
    the flowing branches;
But the trees have become small among
    the new houses,
And will be cut down;
Their beauty cannot save them.

$\mathbf{A}$ STAR rides the twilight now,
All heaven to itself.

...THE altar blazes. I bring
My thoughts to heap upon it.
The smoke of my breath
Is an offering.

Whatever unfriendly stars and comets do,
Whatever stormy heavens are unfurled,
My spirit be like fire in this, too,
That all the straws and rubbish of the world
Only feed its flame.
The seasons change.
That is change enough.

Chance planted me beside a stream of water;
Content, I serve the land,
Whoever lives here and whoever passes.

> This Space for Your
> Thoughts

THE OLD EXPRESSIONS ARE WITH US ALWAYS
AND THERE ARE ALWAYS OTHERS

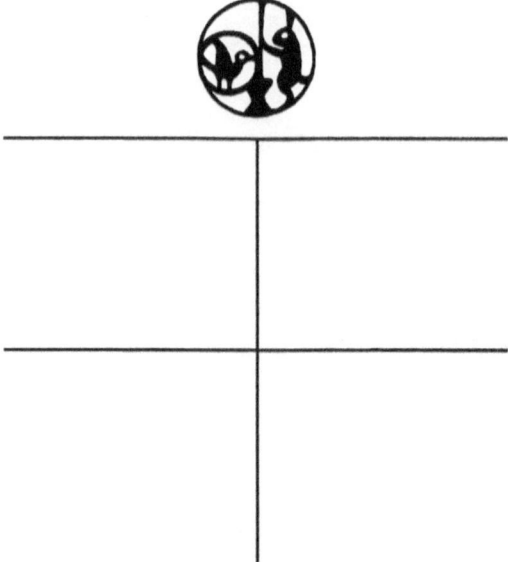

Please handle with care.